D1006211

Poems of Nature

Poems of Nature

Edited by Gail Harvey

GRAMERCY BOOKS
New York • Avenel, New Jersey

Copyright © 1989 by Outlet Book Company, Inc.
All rights reserved.
First published in 1989 by Gramercy Books, distributed by
Outlet Book Company, Inc., a Random House Company,
40 Engelhard Avenue, Avenel, New Jersey 07001.
Manufactured in Singapore

Designed by Don Bender

Library of Congress Cataloging-in-Publication Data

Poems of nature / edited by Gail Harvey.
   p. cm.
  ISBN 0-517-69202-3
  1. Nature—Poetry. 2. English poetry. 3. American
poetry.
I. Harvey, Gail.
PN6110.N2P47 1989   89-32975
808.81'36—dc20   CIP

10 9 8 7 6

Contents

Introduction

"The poetry of earth is never dead," wrote John Keats, and, indeed, it is Nature, the poetry of earth, that brings beauty into our lives, that forces us to change our plans, that affects our moods. Nature sets a sky aflame at sunset, magically transforms a familiar landscape into a snow-white wonderland, paints a clump of daffodils with the glow of soft sunlight. Nature is also responsible for cold, blustery winds, for torrential rain storms, for the cruel heat of high summer. Nature is truly an intrinsic part of our lives. It is no surprise that poets have always written of her charms and her harshness and of the cyclical changes in the natural world around us.

Poems of Nature is a new collection of evocative poetry written by some of the world's greatest poets. Henry Wadsworth Longfellow, for example, writes memorably of snowflakes ". . . the poem of the air, Slowly in silent syllables recorded." Joyously, Pierre Ronsard welcomes the return of spring and in *To The Dandelion* James Russell Lowell declares "Dear common flower, that grow'st beside the way . . . thou art more dear to me than all the prouder summer-blooms may be." Felicia Hemans tells us, in *Willow Song*, what the whispering leaves say and Alfred Tennyson imaginatively records the song of a brook. Helen Hunt Jackson recounts the magic of "October's bright blue weather" and John Greenleaf Whittier writes enchantingly of Indian summer. Included, too, are poems by such wonderful writers as Ralph Waldo Emerson, William Blake, John Milton, William Shakespeare, Christina Rossetti, and John Keats.

The poems in this anthology capture Nature's moods and majesty. They evoke memories and dreams, sadness and laughter. *Poems of Nature* is a celebration of the changing seasons and the natural beauty that is everywhere.

GAIL HARVEY

NEW YORK
1989

A SONG FOR THE SEASONS

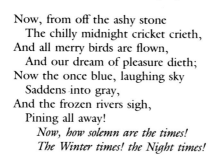

When the merry lark doth gild
  With his song the summer hours,
And their nests the swallows build
  In the roofs and tops of towers,
And the golden broom-flower burns
  All about the waste,
And the maiden May returns
  With a pretty haste,—
    Then, how merry are the times!
    The Summer times! the Spring times!

Now, from off the ashy stone
  The chilly midnight cricket crieth,
And all merry birds are flown,
  And our dream of pleasure dieth;
Now the once blue, laughing sky
  Saddens into gray,
And the frozen rivers sigh,
  Pining all away!
    Now, how solemn are the times!
    The Winter times! the Night times!

Yet, be merry: all around
  Is through one vast change revolving:
Even Night, who lately frowned,
  Is in paler dawn dissolving.
Earth will burst her fetters strange,
  And in Spring grow free;
All things in the world will change,
  Save—my love for thee!
    Sing then, hopeful are all times!
    Winter, Summer, Spring times!

BARRY CORNWALL

WINTER SONG

Summer joys are o'er;
　Flowerets bloom no more,
Wintry winds are sweeping;
Through the snow-drifts peeping,
　Cheerful evergreen
　Rarely now is seen.

　Now no pluméd throng
　　Charms the wood with song;
Ice-bound trees are glittering;
Merry snow-birds, twittering,
　　Fondly strive to cheer
　　Scenes so cold and drear.

　Winter, still I see
　　Many charms in thee,—
Love thy chilly greeting,
Snow-storms fiercely beating,
　　And the dear delights
　　Of the long, long nights.

Ludwig Hölty
*Translated from the
German by Charles T. Brooks*

WINTER MEMORIES

Within the circuit of this plodding life
There enter moments of an azure hue,
Untarnished fair as is the violet
Or anemone, when the spring strews them
By some meandering rivulet, which make
The best philosophy untrue that aims
But to console man for his grievances.
I have remembered when the winter came,
High in my chamber in the frosty nights,
When in the still light of the cheerful moon,
On every twig and rail and jutting spout,
The icy spears were adding to their length
Against the arrows of the coming sun,
How in the shimmering noon of summer past
Some unrecorded beam slanted across
The upland pastures where the Johnswort grew;
Or heard, amid the verdure of my mind,
The bee's long smothered hum, on the blue flag
Loitering amidst the mead; or busy rill,
Which now through all its course stands still
        and dumb
Its own memorial,—purling at its play
Along the slopes, and through the meadows next,
Until its youthful sound was hushed at last
In the staid current of the lowland stream;
Or seen the furrows shine but late upturned,
And where the fieldfare followed in the rear,
When all the fields around lay bound and hoar
Beneath a thick integument of snow.
So by God's cheap economy made rich
To go upon my winter's task again.

HENRY DAVID THOREAU

THE SNOW-STORM

Announced by all the trumpets of the sky,
Arrives the snow, and, driving o'er the fields,
Seems nowhere to alight: the whited air
Hides hills and woods, the river, and the heaven,
And veils the farm-house at the garden's end.
The sled and traveller stopped, the courier's feet
Delayed, all friends shut out, the housemates sit
Around the radiant fireplace, enclosed
In a tumultuous privacy of storm.

Come see the north wind's masonry.
Out of an unseen quarry evermore
Furnished with tile, the fierce artificer
Curves his white bastions with projected roof
Round every windward stake, or tree, or door.
Speeding, the myriad-handed, his wild work
So fanciful, so savage, naught cares he
For number or proportion. Mockingly,
On coop or kennel he hangs Parian wreaths;
A swan-like form invests the hidden thorn;
Fills up the farmer's lane from wall to wall,
Maugre the farmer's sighs; and, at the gate,
A tapering turret overtops the work.
And when his hours are numbered, and the world
Is all his own, retiring, as he were not,
Leaves, when the sun appears, astonished Art
To mimic in slow structures, stone by stone,
Built in an age, the mad wind's nightwork,
The frolic architecture of the snow.

RALPH WALDO EMERSON

SNOW-FLAKES

Out of the bosom of the Air,
  Out of the cloud-folds of her garments shaken,
Over the woodlands brown and bare,
  Over the harvest-fields forsaken,
    Silent and soft and slow
    Descends the snow.

Even as our cloudy fancies take
  Suddenly shape in some divine expression,
Even as the troubled heart doth make
  In the white countenance confession,
    The troubled sky reveals
    The grief it feels.

This is the poem of the air,
  Slowly in silent syllables recorded;
This is the secret of despair,
  Long in its cloudy bosom hoarded,
    Now whispered and revealed
    To wood and field.

HENRY WADSWORTH LONGFELLOW

AFTERNOON IN FEBRUARY

*T*he day is ending
The night is descending;
The marsh is frozen,
   The river dead.

Through clouds like ashes
The red sun flashes
On village windows
   That glimmer red.

The snow recommences;
The buried fences
Mark no longer
   The road o'er the plain;

While through the meadows,
Like fearful shadows,
Slowly passes
   A funeral train.

The bell is pealing,
And every feeling
Within me responds
   To the dismal knell;

Shadows are trailing,
My heart is bewailing
And tolling within
   Like a funeral bell.

HENRY WADSWORTH LONGFELLOW

BLOW, BLOW, THOU
WINTER WIND

Blow, blow, thou winter wind—
Thou art not so unkind
  As man's ingratitude;
Thy tooth is not so keen,
Because thou art not seen,
  Although thy breath be rude.
Heigh ho! sing heigh ho! unto the green
      holly:
Most friendship is feigning, most loving mere
      folly;
  Then, heigh ho! the holly!
  This life is most jolly.

Freeze, freeze, thou bitter sky—
Thou dost not bite so nigh
  As benefits forgot;
Though thou the waters warp,
Thy sting is not so sharp
  As friend remembered not.
Heigh ho! sing heigh ho! unto the green
      holly:
Most friendship is feigning, most loving mere
      folly;
  Then, heigh ho! the holly!
  This life is most jolly!

WILLIAM SHAKESPEARE

WHEN THE HOUNDS
OF SPRING

When the hounds of spring are on winter's traces,
   The mother of months in meadow or plain
Fills the shadows and windy places
   With lisp of leaves and ripple of rain;
And the brown bright nightingale amorous
Is half assuaged for Itylus,
For the Thracian ships and the foreign faces;
   The tongueless vigil, and all the pain.

Come with bows bent and with emptying of quivers,
   Maiden most perfect, lady of light,
With a noise of winds and many rivers,
   With a clamor of waters, and with might;
Bind on thy sandals, O thou most fleet,
Over the splendor and speed of thy feet!
For the faint east quickens, the wan west shivers,
   Round the feet of the day and the feet of the
      night.

Where shall we find her, how shall we sing to her,
   Fold our hands round her knees and cling?
O that man's heart were as fire and could spring
      to her,
   Fire, or the strength of the streams that spring!
For the stars and the winds are unto her
As raiment, as songs of the harp-player;
For the risen stars and the fallen cling to her,
   And the southwest-wind and the west-wind
      sing.

For winter's rains and ruins are over,
    And all the season of snows and sins;
The days dividing lover and lover,
    The light that loses, the night that wins;
And time remembered is grief forgotten,
And frosts are slain and flowers begotten,
And in green underwood and cover
    Blossom by blossom the spring begins.

The full streams feed on flower of rushes,
    Ripe grasses trammel a travelling foot,
The faint fresh flame of the young year flushes
    From leaf to flower and flower to fruit;
And fruit and leaf are as gold and fire,
And the oat is heard above the lyre,
And the hoofèd heel of a satyr crushes
    The chestnut-husk at the chestnut-root.

And Pan by noon and Bacchus by night,
    Fleeter of foot than the fleet-foot kid,
Follows with dancing and fills with delight
    The Maenad and the Bassarid;
And soft as lips that laugh and hide,
The laughing leaves of the trees divide,
And screen from seeing and leave in sight
    The god pursuing, the maiden hid.

The ivy falls with the Bacchanal's hair
    Over her eyebrows shading her eyes;
The wild vine slipping down leaves bare
    Her bright breast shortening into sighs;
The wild vine slips with the weight of its leaves,
But the berried ivy catches and cleaves
To the limbs that glitter, the feet that scare
    The wolf that follows, the fawn that flies.

ALGERNON CHARLES SWINBURNE

MARCH

*T*he cock is crowing,
　The stream is flowing,
　The small birds twitter,
　The lake doth glitter,
The green field sleeps in the sun;
　The oldest and youngest
　Are at work with the strongest;
　The cattle are grazing,
　Their heads never raising;
There are forty feeding like one!

　Like an army defeated
　The snow hath retreated,
　And now doth fare ill
　On the top of the bare hill;
The plough-boy is whooping—anon—anon!
　There's joy on the mountains;
　There's life in the fountains;
　Small clouds are sailing,
　Blue sky prevailing;
The rain is over and gone!

WILLIAM WORDSWORTH

RETURN OF SPRING

Translated from the French

God shield ye, heralds of the spring,
Ye faithful swallows, fleet of wing,
　　Houps, cuckoos, nightingales,
Turtles, and every wilder bird,
That make your hundred chirpings heard
　　Through the green woods and dales.

God shield ye, Easter daisies all,
Fair roses, buds, and blossoms small,
　　And he whom erst the gore
Of Ajax and Narciss did print,
Ye wild thyme, anise, balm, and mint,
　　I welcome ye once more.

God shield ye, bright embroidered train
Of butterflies, that on the plain
　　Of each sweet herblet sip;
And ye, new swarms of bees, that go
Where the pink flowers and yellow grow
　　To kiss them with your lip.

A hundred thousand times I call
A hearty welcome on ye all;
　　This season how I love—
This merry din on every shore—
For winds and storms, whose sullen roar
　　Forbade my steps to rove.

PIERRE RONSARD

TO THE REDBREAST

Sweet bird! that sing'st away the early
    hours
Of winters past or coming, void of care.
Well pleased with delights which present are,
Fair seasons, budding sprays, sweet-smelling
    flowers—
To rocks, to springs, to rills, from leafy
    bowers
Thou thy Creator's goodness dost declare,
And what dear gifts on thee he did not spare,
A stain to human sense in sin that lowers.
What soul can be so sick which by thy songs
(Attired in sweetness) sweetly is not driven
Quite to forget earth's turmoils, spites, and
    wrongs,
And lift a reverend eye and thought to
    Heaven!
Sweet, artless songster! thou my mind dost
    raise
To airs of spheres—yes, and to angels' lays.

WILLIAM DRUMMOND

TO SPRING

O Thou with dewy locks, who lookest down
Through the clear windows of the morning, turn
Thine angel eyes upon our western isle,
Which in full choir hails thy approach, O Spring!

The hills tell one another, and the listening
Valleys hear; all our longing eyes are turned
Up to thy bright pavilions: issue forth
And let thy holy feet visit our clime!

Come o'er the eastern hills, and let our winds
Kiss thy perfumed garments; let us taste
Thy morn and evening breath; scatter thy pearls
Upon our lovesick land that mourns for thee.

O deck her forth with thy fair fingers; pour
Thy soft kisses on her bosom; and put
Thy golden crown upon her languished head,
Whose modest tresses are bound up for thee!

WILLIAM BLAKE

APRIL

I have found violets. April hath come on,
And the cool winds feel softer, and the rain
Falls in the beaded drops of summer time.
You may hear birds at morning, and at eve
The tame dove lingers till the twilight falls,
Cooing upon the eaves, and drawing in
His beautiful bright neck, and, from the hills,
A murmur like the hoarseness of the sea
Tells the release of waters, and the earth
Sends up a pleasant smell, and the dry leaves
Are lifted by the grass; and so I know
That Nature, with her delicate ear, hath heard
The dropping of the velvet foot of Spring.
Take of my violets! I found them where
The liquid South stole o'er them, on a bank
That leaned to running water. There's to me
A daintiness about these early flowers
That touches me like poetry. They blow
With such a simple loveliness among
The common herbs of pasture, and breathe out
Their lives so unobtrusively, like hearts
Whose beatings are too gentle for the world.

I love to go in the capricious days
Of April and hung violets; when the rain
Is in the blue cups trembling, and they nod
So gracefully to the kisses of the wind.
It may be deem'd too idle, but the young
Read nature like the manuscript of heaven,
And call the flowers its poetry. Go out!
Ye spirits of habitual unrest,
And read it when the "fever·of the world"
Hath made your hearts impatient, and, if life
Hath yet one spring unpoisoned, it will be
Like a beguiling music to its flow,
And you will no more wonder that I love
To hunt for violets in the April time.

NATHANIEL PARKER WILLIS

MAY MORNING

Now the bright morning star, day's harbinger,
Comes dancing from the east, and leads with her
The flowery May, who from her green lap throws
The yellow cowslip and the pale primrose.
Hail, bounteous May! that doth inspire
Mirth and youth and warm desire;
Woods and groves are of thy dressing,
Hill and dale doth boast thy blessing.
Thus we salute thee with our early song,
And welcome thee, and wish thee long.

JOHN MILTON

SPRING QUIET

Gone were but the Winter,
   Come were but the Spring,
I would go to a covert
   Where the birds sing;

Where in the whitethorn
   Singeth a thrush,
And a robin sings
   In the holly-bush.

Full of fresh scents
   Are the budding boughs
Arching high over
   A cool green house;

Full of sweet scents,
   And whispering air
Which sayeth softly:
   "We spread no snare;

"Here dwell in safety,
   Here dwell alone,
With a clear stream
   And a mossy stone.

"Here the sun shineth
   Most shadily;
Here is heard an echo
   Of the far sea,
     Though far off it be."

CHRISTINA ROSSETTI

THE RHODORA

On Being Asked, Whence Is the Flower?

In May, when sea-winds pierced our solitudes,
I found the fresh Rhodora in the woods,
Spreading its leafless blooms in a damp nook,
To please the desert and the sluggish brook.
The purple petals, fallen in the pool,
Made the black water with their beauty gay;
Here might the red-bird come his plumes to cool,
And court the flower that cheapens his array.
Rhodora! if the sages ask thee why
This charm is wasted on the earth and sky,
Tell them, dear, that if eyes were made for seeing,
Then Beauty is its own excuse for being:
Why thou wert there, O rival of the rose!
I never thought to ask, I never knew;
But, in my simple ignorance, suppose
The self-same Power that brought me there brought you.

RALPH WALDO EMERSON

DAFFODILS

I wandered lonely as a cloud
   That floats on high o'er vales and hills,
When all at once I saw a crowd,—
   A host of golden daffodils
Beside the lake, beneath the trees,
Fluttering and dancing in the breeze.

Continuous as the stars that shine
   And twinkle on the Milky Way,
They stretched in never-ending line
   Along the margin of a bay:
Ten thousand saw I, at a glance,
Tossing their heads in sprightly dance.

The waves beside them danced, but they
   Outdid the sparkling waves in glee;
A poet could not but be gay
   In such a jocund company;
I gazed—and gazed—but little thought
What wealth the show to me had brought.

For oft, when on my couch I lie,
   In vacant or in pensive mood,
They flash upon that inward eye
   Which is the bliss of solitude;
And then my heart with pleasure fills,
And dances with the daffodils.

WILLIAM WORDSWORTH

TO THE DANDELION

$\mathcal{D}$ear common flower, that grow'st beside the way,
Fringing the dusty road with harmless gold!
   First pledge of blithesome May,
Which children pluck, and, full of pride, uphold—
  High-hearted buccaneers, o'erjoyed that they
An Eldorado in the grass have found,
  Which not the rich earth's ample round
May match in wealth!—thou art more dear to me
Than all the prouder summer-blooms may be.

  Gold such as thine ne'er drew the Spanish prow
Through the primeval hush of Indian seas;
   Nor wrinkled the lean brow
Of age, to rob the lover's heart of ease.
'Tis the Spring's largess, which she scatters now
To rich and poor alike, with lavish hand,
  Though most hearts never understand
  To take it at God's value, but pass by
The offered wealth with unrewarded eye.

  Thou art my tropics and mine Italy;
To look at thee unlocks a warmer clime;
   The eyes thou givest me
Are in the heart, and heed not space or time:
  Not in mid June the golden-cuirassed bee
Feels a more summer-like, warm ravishment
   In the white lily's breezy tent,
  His conquered Sybaris, than I, when first
  From the dark green thy yellow circles burst.

Then think I of deep shadows on the grass;
Of meadows where in sun the cattle graze,
    Where, as the breezes pass,
The gleaming rushes lean a thousand ways;
    Of leaves that slumber in a cloudy mass,
Or whiten in the wind; of waters blue,
        That from the distance sparkle through
    Some woodland gap; and of a sky above,
    Where one white cloud like a stray lamb doth move.

My childhood's earliest thoughts are linked with thee;
The sight of thee calls back the robin's song,
    Who, from the dark old tree
Beside the door, sang clearly all day long;
    And I, secure in childish piety,
Listened as if I heard an angel sing
        With news from heaven, which he did bring
    Fresh every day to my untainted ears,
    When birds and flowers and I were happy peers.

How like a prodigal doth nature seem,
When thou, for all thy gold, so common art!
    Thou teachest me to deem
More sacredly of every human heart,
    Since each reflects in joy its scanty gleam
Of heaven, and could some wondrous secret show,
        Did we but pay the love we owe,
    And with a child's undoubting wisdom look
    On all these living pages of God's book.

JAMES RUSSELL LOWELL

THE DAISY

*T*here is a flower, a little flower
   With silver crest and golden eye,
That welcomes every changing hour,
   And weathers every sky.

The prouder beauties of the field
   In gay but quick succession shine;
Race after race their honors yield,
   They flourish and decline.

But this small flower, to Nature dear,
   While moons and stars their courses run,
Inwreathes the circle of the year,
   Companion of the sun.

It smiles upon the lap of May,
   To sultry August spreads its charm,
Lights pale October on his way,
   And twines December's arm.

The purple heath and golden broom
   On moory mountains catch the gale;
O'er lawns the lily sheds perfume,
   The violet in the vale.

But this bold floweret climbs the hill,
   Hides in the forest, haunts the glen,
Plays on the margin of the rill,
   Peeps round the fox's den.

Within the garden's cultured round
   It shares the sweet carnation's bed;
And blooms on consecrated ground
   In honor of the dead.

The lambkin crops its crimson gem;
   The wild bee murmurs on its breast;
The blue-fly bends its pensile stem
   Light o'er the skylark's nest.

'Tis Flora's page,—in every place,
   In every season, fresh and fair;
It opens with perennial grace,
   And blossoms everywhere.

On waste and woodland, rock and plain,
   Its humble buds unheeded rise;
The rose has but a summer reign;
   The daisy never dies!

JAMES MONTGOMERY

THEY COME! THE MERRY
SUMMER MONTHS

*T*hey come! the merry summer months of
    beauty, song, and flowers;
They come! the gladsome months that bring
    thick leafiness to bowers.
Up, up, my heart! and walk abroad; fling cark
    and care aside;
Seek silent hills, or rest thyself where peaceful
    waters glide;
Or, underneath the shadow vast of patriarchal
    tree,
Scan through its leaves the cloudless sky in rapt
    tranquillity.

The grass is soft, its velvet touch is grateful to
    the hand;
And, like the kiss of maiden love, the breeze is
    sweet and bland;
The daisy and the buttercup are nodding
    courteously;
It stirs their blood with kindest love, to bless
    and welcome thee;
And mark how with thine own thin locks—
    they now are silvery gray—
That blissful breeze is wantoning, and whisper-
    ing, "Be gay!"

There is no cloud that sails along the ocean of
    yon sky
But hath its own winged mariners to give lit
    melody;
Thou seest their glittering fans outspread, all
    gleaming like red gold;
And hark! with shrill pipe musical, their merry
    course they hold.
God bless them all, those little ones, who, far
    above this earth,
Can make a scoff of its mean joys, and vent a
    nobler mirth.

But soft! mine ear upcaught a sound,—from
    yonder wood it came!
The spirit of the dim green glade did breathe his
    own glad name;—
Yes, it is he! the hermit bird, that, apart from
    all his kind,
Slow spells his beads monotonous to the soft
    western wind;
Cuckoo! Cuckoo! he sings again,—his notes are
    void of art;
But simplest strains do soonest sound the deep
    founts of the heart.

Good Lord! it is a gracious boon for thought-
    crazed wight like me,
To smell again these summer flowers beneath this
    summer tree!
To suck once more in every breath their little
    souls away,
And feed my fancy with fond dreams of youth's
    bright summer day,
When, rushing forth like untamed colt,
    the reckless, truant boy
Wandered through greenwoods all day long, a
    mighty heart of joy!

I'm sadder now,—I have had cause; but O,
    I'm proud to think
That each pure joy-fount, loved of yore, I yet
    delight to drink;—
Leaf, blossom, blade, hill, valley, stream, the
    calm, unclouded sky,
Still mingle music with my dreams, as in the
    days gone by.
When summer's loveliness and light fall round
    me dark and cold,
I'll bear indeed life's heaviest curse,—a heart
    that hath waxed old!

WILLIAM MOTHERWELL

SUMMER MORNING

From "The Seasons"

Short is the doubtful empire of the night;
And soon, observant of approaching day,
The meek-eyed morn appears, mother of dews,
At first faint gleaming in the dappled east,—
Till far o'er ether spreads the widening glow,
And, from before the lustre of her face,
White break the clouds away. With quickened
    step,
Brown night retires. Young day pours in apace,
And opens all the lawny prospect wide.
The dripping rock, the mountain's misty top,
Swell on the sight, and brighten with the dawn.
Blue, through the dusk, the smoking currents
    shine;
And from the bladed field the fearful hare
Limps, awkward; while along the forest glade
The wild deer trip, and often turning gaze
At early passenger. Music awakes,
The native voice of undissembled joy;
And thick around the woodland hymns arise.
Roused by the cock, the soon-clad shepherd leaves
His mossy cottage, where with peace he dwells;
And from the crowded fold, in order, drives
His flock, to taste the verdure of the morn.

JAMES THOMSON

SONG OF THE SUMMER WINDS

Up the dale and down the bourne,
  O'er the meadow swift we fly;
Now we sing, and now we mourn,
  Now we whistle, now we sigh.

By the grassy-fringéd river,
  Through the murmuring reeds we sweep;
Mid the lily-leaves we quiver,
  To their very hearts we creep.

Now the maiden rose is blushing
  At the frolic things we say,
While aside her cheek we're rushing,
  Like some truant bees at play.

Through the blooming groves we rustle,
  Kissing every bud we pass,—
As we did it in the bustle,
  Scarcely knowing how it was.

Down the glen, across the mountain,
  O'er the yellow heath we roam,
Whirling round about the fountain,
  Till its little breakers foam.

Bending down the weeping willows,
  While our vesper hymn we sigh;
Then unto our rosy pillows
  On our weary wings we hie.

There of idlenesses dreaming,
  Scarce from waking we refrain,
Moments long as ages deeming
  Till we're at our play again.

GEORGE DARLEY

A JUNE DAY

Who has not dreamed a world of bliss
On a bright sunny noon like this,
Couched by his native brook's green maze,
With comrade of his boyish days,
While all around them seemed to be
Just as in joyous infancy?
Who has not loved at such an hour,
Upon that heath, in birchen bower,
Lulled in the poet's dreamy mood,
Its wild and sunny solitude?
While o'er the waste of purple ling
You mark a sultry glimmering;
Silence herself there seems to sleep,
Wrapped in a slumber long and deep,
Where slowly stray those lonely sheep
Through the tall foxglove's crimson bloom,
And gleaming of the scattered broom.
Love you not, then, to list and hear
The crackling of the gorse-flowers near,
Pouring an orange-scented tide
Of fragrance o'er the desert wide?
To hear the buzzard's whimpering shrill,
Hovering above you high and still?
The twittering of the bird that dwells
Among the heath's delicious bells?
While round your bed, o'er fern and blade,
Insects in green and gold arrayed,
The sun's gay tribes have lightly strayed;
And sweeter sound their humming wings
Than the proud minstrel's echoing strings.

WILLIAM HOWITT

SUMMER MOODS

I love at eventide to walk alone,
Down narrow glens, o'erhung with dewy thorn,
Where, from the long grass underneath, the snail,
Jet black, creeps out, and sprouts his timid horn.
I love to muse o'er meadows newly mown,
Where withering grass perfumes the sultry air;
Where bees search round, with sad and weary
    drone,
In vain, for flowers that bloomed but newly
    there;
While in the juicy corn the hidden quail
Cries, "Wet my foot"; and, hid as thoughts
    unborn,
The fairy-like and seldom-seen land-rail
Utters "Craik, craik," like voices underground,
Right glad to meet the evening's dewy veil,
And see the light fade into gloom around.

JOHN CLARE

MOONLIGHT IN SUMMER

Low on the utmost boundary of the sight,
The rising vapors catch the silver light;
Thence fancy measures, as they parting fly,
Which first will throw its shadow on the eye,
Passing the source of light; and thence away,
Succeeded quick by brighter still than they.
For yet above these wafted clouds are seen
(In a remoter sky still more serene)
Others, detached in ranges through the air,
Spotless as snow, and countless as they're fair;
Scattered immensely wide from east to west,
The beauteous semblance of a flock at rest.
These, to the raptured mind, aloud proclaim
Their mighty Shepherd's everlasting name;
And thus the loiterer's utmost stretch of soul
Climbs the still clouds, or passes those that roll,
And loosed imagination soaring goes
High o'er his home and all his little woes.

ROBERT BLOOMFIELD

GREEN RIVER

When breezes are soft and skies are fair,
I steal an hour from study and care,
And hie me away to the woodland scene,
Where wanders the stream with waters of green,
As if the bright fringe of herbs on its brink
Had given their stain to the waves they drink;
And they, whose meadows it murmurs through,
Have named the stream from its own fair hue.

Yet pure its waters—its shallows are bright
With colored pebbles and sparkles of light,
And clear the depths where its eddies play,
And dimples deepen and whirl away,
And the plane-tree's speckled arms o'ershoot
The swifter current that mines its root,
Through whose shifting leaves, as you walk the hill,
The quivering glimmer of sun and rill
With a sudden flash on the eye is thrown,
Like the ray that streams from the diamond-stone.
Oh, loveliest there the spring days come,
With blossoms, and birds, and wild-bees' hum;
The flowers of summer are fairest there,
And freshest the breath of the summer air;
And sweetest the golden autumn day
In silence and sunshine glides away.

Yet, fair as thou art, thou shunnest to glide,
Beautiful stream! by the village side;
But windest away from haunts of men,
To quiet valley and shaded glen;
And forest, and meadow, and slope of hill,
Around thee, are lonely, lovely, and still,
Lonely—save when, by thy rippling tides,
From thicket to thicket the angler glides;
Or the simpler comes, with basket and book,
For herbs of power on thy banks to look;

Or haply, some idle dreamer, like me,
To wander, and muse, and gaze on thee,
Still—save the chirp of birds that feed
On the river cherry and seedy reed,
And thy own wild music gushing out
With mellow murmur of fairy shout,
From dawn to the blush of another day,
Like traveller singing along his way.

That fairy music I never hear,
Nor gaze on those waters so green and clear,
And mark them winding away from sight,
Darkened with shade or flashing with light,
While o'er them the vine to its thicket clings,
And the zephyr stoops to freshen his wings,
But I wish that fate had left me free
To wander these quiet haunts with thee,
Till the eating cares of earth should depart,
And the peace of the scene pass into my heart;
And I envy thy stream, as it glides along
Through its beautiful banks in a trance of song.

Though forced to drudge for the dregs of men,
And scrawl strange words with the barbarous pen,
And mingle among the jostling crowd,
Where the sons of strife are subtle and loud—
I often come to this quiet place,
To breathe the airs that ruffle thy face,
And gaze upon thee in silent dream,
For in thy lonely and lovely stream
An image of that calm life appears
That won my heart in my greener years.

WILLIAM CULLEN BRYANT

JULY

Loud is the Summer's busy song,
The smallest breeze can find a tongue,
While insects of each tiny size
Grow teasing with their melodies,
Till noon burns with its blistering breath
Around, and day lies still as death.

The busy noise of man and brute
Is on a sudden lost and mute;
Even the brook that leaps along,
Seems weary of its bubbling song.
And, so soft its waters creep,
Tired silence sinks in sounder sleep;

The cricket on its bank is dumb;
The very flies forget to hum;
And, save the wagon rocking round,
The landscape sleeps without a sound.
The breeze is stopped, the lazy bough
Hath not a leaf that danceth now;

The taller grass upon the hill,
And spider's threads, are standing still;
The feathers, dropped from moorhen's wing,
Which to the water's surface cling,
Are steadfast, and as heavy seem
As stones beneath them in the stream;

Hawkweed and groundsel's fanny downs
Unruffled keep their seedy crowns;
And in the over-heated air
Not one light thing is floating there,
Save that to the earnest eye
The restless heat seems twittering by.

Noon swoons beneath the heat it made,
And flowers e'en within the shade;
Until the sun slopes in the west,
Like weary traveller, glad to rest
On pillowed clouds of many hues.
Then Nature's voice its joy renews,

And checkered field and grassy plain
Hum with their summer songs again,
A requiem to the day's decline,
Whose setting sunbeams coolly shine
As welcome to day's feeble powers
As falling dews to thirsty flowers.

JOHN CLARE

THE VOICE OF THE GRASS

Here I come creeping, creeping everywhere;
    By the dusty roadside,
    On the sunny hillside,
    Close by the noisy brook
    In every shady nook,
I come creeping, creeping everywhere.

Here I come creeping, smiling everywhere;
    All round the open door,
    Where sit the aged poor;
    Here where the children play,
    In the bright and merry May,
I come creeping, creeping everywhere.

Here I come creeping, creeping everywhere;
    In the noisy city street
    My pleasant face you'll meet,
    Cheering the sick at heart
    Toiling his busy part,—
Silently creeping, creeping everywhere.

Here I come creeping, creeping everywhere;
    You cannot see me coming,
    Nor hear my low sweet humming;
    For in the starry night,
    And the glad morning light,
I come quietly creeping everywhere.

Here I come creeping, creeping everywhere;
    More welcome than the flowers
    In summer's pleasant hours;
    The gentle cow is glad,
    And the merry bird not sad,
To see me creeping, creeping everywhere.

Here I come creeping, creeping everywhere;
    When you're numbered with the dead
    In your still and narrow bed,
    In the happy spring I'll come
    And deck your silent home,—
Creeping, silently creeping everywhere.

Here I come creeping, creeping everywhere;
    My humble song of praise
    Most joyfully I raise
    To Him at whose command
    I beautify the land,
Creeping, silently creeping everywhere.

SARAH ROBERTS

WILLOW SONG

Willow! in thy breezy moan
I can hear a deeper tone;
Through thy leaves come whispering low
Faint sweet sounds of long ago—
                    Willow, sighing willow!

Many a mournful tale of old
Heart-sick Love to thee hath told,
Gathering from thy golden bough
Leaves to cool his burning brow—
                    Willow, sighing willow!

Many a swan-like song to thee
Hath been sung, thou gentle tree;
Many a lute its last lament
Down thy moonlight stream hath sent—
                    Willow, sighing willow!

Therefore, wave and murmur on,
Sigh for sweet affections gone,
And for tuneful voices fled,
And for Love, whose heart hath bled,
                    Ever, willow, willow!

FELICIA HEMANS

THE GRASSHOPPER AND CRICKET

The poetry of earth is never dead;
When all the birds are faint with the hot sun
And hide in cooling trees, a voice will run
From hedge to hedge about the new-mown mead.
That is the grasshopper's,—he takes the lead
In summer luxury,—he has never done
With his delights; for, when tired out with fun,
He rests at ease beneath some pleasant weed.
The poetry of earth is ceasing never.
On a lone winter evening, when the frost
Has wrought a silence, from the stove there shrills
The cricket's song, in warmth increasing ever,
And seems, to one in drowsiness half lost,
The grasshopper's among some grassy hills.

JOHN KEATS

SONG OF THE BROOK

I come from haunts of coot and hern:
　　I make a sudden sally
And sparkle out among the fern,
　　To bicker down a valley.

By thirty hills I hurry down,
　　Or slip between the ridges,
By twenty thorps, a little town,
　　And half a hundred bridges.

Till last by Philip's farm I flow
　　To join the brimming river,
For men may come and men may go,
　　But I go on forever.

I chatter over stony ways,
　　In little sharps and trebles,
I bubble into eddying bays,
　　I babble on the pebbles.

With many a curve my banks I fret
　　By many a field and fallow,
And many a fairy foreland set
　　With willow-weed and mallow.

I chatter, chatter, as I flow
　　To join the brimming river;
For men may come and men may go,
　　But I go on forever.

I wind about, and in and out,
  With here a blossom sailing,
And here and there a lusty trout,
  And here and there a grayling,

And here and there a foamy flake
  Upon me, as I travel
With many a silvery waterbreak
  Above the golden gravel,

And draw them all along, and flow
  To join the brimming river,
For men may come and men may go,
  But I go on forever.

I steal by lawns and grassy plots:
  I slide by hazel covers;
I move the sweet forget-me-nots
  That grow for happy lovers.

I slip, I slide, I gloom, I glance,
  Among my skimming swallows:
I make the netted sunbeam dance
  Against my sandy shallows.

I murmur under moon and stars
  In brambly wildernesses;
I linger by my shingly bars;
  I loiter round my cresses;

And out again I curve and flow
  To join the brimming river,
For men may come and men may go,
  But I go on forever.

ALFRED TENNYSON

ODE TO AUTUMN

Season of mists and mellow fruitfulness!
Close bosom-friend of the maturing sun;
Conspiring with him how to load and bless
With fruit the vines that round the thatch-eaves run;
To bend with apples the moss'd cottage-trees,
And fill all fruit with ripeness to the core;
To swell the gourd, and plump the hazel shells
With a sweet kernel; to set budding more
And still more, later flowers for the bees,
Until they think warm days will never cease;
For Summer has o'erbrimm'd their clammy cells.

Who hath not seen Thee oft amid thy store?
Sometimes whoever seeks abroad may find
Thee sitting careless on a granary floor,
Thy hair soft-lifted by the winnowing wind;
Or on a half-reap'd furrow sound asleep,
Drowsed with the fume of poppies, while thy hook
Spares the next swath and all its twinéd flowers;
And sometimes like a gleaner thou dost keep
Steady thy laden head across a brook;
Or by a cider-press, with patient look,
Thou watchest the last oozings, hours by hours.

Where are the songs of Spring? Aye, where are they?
Think not of them,—thou hast thy music too,
While barréd clouds bloom the soft-dying day
And touch the stubble-plains with rosy hue;
Then in a wailful choir the small gnats mourn
Among the river-sallows, borne aloft
Or sinking as the light wind lives or dies;
And full-grown lambs loud bleat from hilly bourn;
Hedge-crickets sing, and now with treble soft
The redbreast whistles from a garden-croft,
And gathering swallows twitter in the skies.

JOHN KEATS

INDIAN SUMMER

From gold to gray
Our mild sweet day
Of Indian summer fades too soon;
But tenderly
Above the sea
Hangs, white and calm, the hunter's moon.

In its pale fire,
The village spire
Shows like the zodiac's spectral lance;
The painted walls
Whereon it falls
Transfigured stand in marble trance!

JOHN GREENLEAF WHITTIER

A SONG FOR SEPTEMBER

September strews the woodland o'er
  With many a brilliant color;
The world is brighter than before—
  Why should our hearts be duller?
Sorrow and the scarlet leaf,
  Sad thoughts and sunny weather!
Ah me! this glory and this grief
  Agree not well together.

This is the parting season—this
  The time when friends are flying;
And lovers now, with many a kiss,
  Their long farewells are sighing.
Why is Earth so gayly drest?
  This pomp, that Autumn beareth,
A funeral seems, where every guest
  A bridal garment weareth.

Each one of us, perchance, may here,
  On some blue morn hereafter,
Return to view the gaudy year,
  But not with boyish laughter.
We shall then be wrinkled men,
  Our brows with silver laden,
And thou this glen may'st seek again,
  But nevermore a maiden!

Nature perhaps foresees that Spring
  Will touch her teeming bosom,
And that a few brief months will bring
  The bird, the bee, the blossom;
Ah! these forests do not know—
  Or would less brightly wither—
The virgin that adorns them so
  Will never more come hither!

Thomas William Parsons

AUTUMN FLOWERS

*T*hose few pale Autumn flowers,
　How beautiful they are!
Than all that went before,
Than all the Summer store,
　How lovelier far!

And why?—They are the last!
　The last! the last! the last!
Oh! by that little word
How many thoughts are stirred
　That whisper of the past!

Pale flowers! pale perishing flowers!
　Ye 're types of precious things;
Types of those bitter moments,
That flit, like life's enjoyments,
　On rapid, rapid wings:

Last hours with parting dear ones,
　(That Time the fastest spends)
Last tears in silence shed,
Last words half uttered,
　Last looks of dying friends.

Who but would fain compress
　　A life into a day,—
The last day spent with one
Who, ere the morrow's sun,
　　Must leave us, and for aye?

O precious, precious moments!
　　Pale flowers! ye 're types of those;
The saddest, sweetest, dearest,
Because, like those, the nearest
　　To an eternal close.

Pale flowers! pale perishing flowers!
　　I woo your gentle breath—
I leave the Summer rose
For younger, blither brows;
　　Tell me of change and death.

Caroline Bowles Southey

TO THE FRINGED GENTIAN

Thou blossom bright with autumn dew,
And colored with the heaven's own blue,
That openest when the quiet light
Succeeds the keen and frosty night.

Thou comest not when violets lean
O'er wandering brooks and springs unseen,
Or columbines, in purple dressed,
Nod o'er the ground-bird's hidden nest.

Thou waitest late and com'st alone,
When woods are bare and birds are flown,
And frosts and shortening days portend
The aged year is near his end.

Then doth thy sweet and quiet eye
Look through its fringes to the sky,
Blue—blue—as if that sky let fall
A flower from its cerulean wall.

I would that thus, when I shall see
The hour of death draw near to me,
Hope, blossoming within my heart,
May look to heaven as I depart.

WILLIAM CULLEN BRYANT

THE LATTER RAIN

The latter rain,—it falls in anxious haste
Upon the sun-dried fields and branches bare,
Loosening with searching drops the rigid
    waste
As if it would each root's lost strength repair;
But not a blade grows green as in the Spring;
No swelling twig puts forth its thickening
    leaves;
The robins only mid the harvests sing,
Pecking the grain that scatters from the
    sheaves;
The rain falls still,—the fruit all ripened
    drops,
It pierces chestnut-burr and walnut-shell;
The furrowed fields disclose the yellow crops;
Each bursting pod of talents used can tell;
And all that once received the early rain
Declare to man it was not sent in vain.

JONES VERY

OCTOBER'S BRIGHT BLUE WEATHER

O suns and skies and clouds of June,
  And flowers of June together,
Ye cannot rival for one hour
  October's bright blue weather.

When loud the humblebee makes haste,
  Belated, thriftless vagrant,
And Golden Rod is dying fast,
  And lanes with grapes are fragrant;

When Gentians roll their fringes tight,
  To save them for the morning,
And chestnuts fall from satin burrs
  Without a sound of warning;

When on the ground red apples lie
  In piles like jewels shining,
And redder still on old stone walls
  Are leaves of woodbine twining;

When all the lovely wayside things
   Their white-winged seeds are sowing,
And in the fields, still green and fair,
   Late aftermaths are growing;

When springs run low, and on the brooks,
   In idle golden freighting,
Bright leaves sink noiseless in the hush
   Of woods, for winter waiting;

When comrades seek sweet country haunts,
   By twos and twos together,
And count like misers, hour by hour,
   October's bright blue weather.

O suns and skies and flowers of June,
   Count all your boasts together,
Love loveth best of all the year
   October's bright blue weather.

HELEN HUNT JACKSON

AUTUMN

The Autumn is old;
The sere leaves are flying;
He hath gathered up gold,
And now he is dying:
Old age, begin sighing!

The vintage is ripe;
The harvest is heaping;
But some that have sowed
Have no riches for reaping:—
Poor wretch, fall a-weeping!

The year's in the wane;
There is nothing adorning;
The night has no eve,
And the day has no morning;
Cold winter gives warning.

The rivers run chill;
The red sun is sinking;
And I am grown old,
And life is fast shrinking;
Here's enow for sad thinking!

THOMAS HOOD

NOVEMBER

The mellow year is hasting to its close;
The little birds have almost sung their last,
Their small notes twitter in the dreary blast—
That shrill-piped harbinger of early snows;
The patient beauty of the scentless rose,
Oft with the morn's hoar crystal quaintly
        glassed,
Hangs, a pale mourner for the summer past,
And makes a little summer where it grows.
In the chill sunbeam of the faint brief day
The dusky waters shudder as they shine;
The russet leaves obstruct the straggling way
Of oozy brooks, which no deep banks define;
And the gaunt woods, in ragged, scant array,
Wrap their old limbs with sombre ivy twine.

HARTLEY COLERIDGE

THE RAINBOW

$\mathcal{M}$y heart leaps up when I behold
    A rainbow in the sky;
So was it when my life began,
So is it now I am a man,
So be it when I shall grow old,
    Or let me die!
The Child is father of the Man;
And I could wish my days to be
Bound each to each by natural piety.

WILLIAM WORDSWORTH